Anatomy of a RIOT

Poetry From The Edge of Violence

Evan McMahon

Liberty Street Press

Library of Congress Control Number: PENDING *(typical
government bureaucracy)*

ISBN: 979-8-88871-004-3
eBook ISBN: 979-8-88871-003-6

Available while supplies last, or until they shut us down.

PRINTED WITHIN THE IMAGEINARY LINES OF A FAILED STATE

Liberty Street Press – Indianapolis, IN

Dedicated to those hapless fools wasting their breath screaming at their TV (or videos in their FYP).

Stop crying and go break shit!

CONTENTS

You just bought, with your fake ass money, a poetic pipe bomb and lit the fuse with violent intention.

This book isn't just a collection—it's a reckoning, a memory, a warning, and a war cry.

If you're looking for healing, it's not here.
But if you're looking for something sharp to carry in your mouth... you found it.

ABOUT THE AUTHOR

Evan McMahon is what happens when you tell a kid to sit down and shut up one too many times.

Born in an Indiana town that called itself a city and raised in the margins of every institution that claimed to care, he grew into a carrier of flames, fragmentation, and fierce independence.

He's protested, organized, got arrested, and fucked and voted like it was an act of war.

His poems live somewhere between that salty taste when your teeth are laying on the bar floor and the memory of that first time holding hands.

He writes for the ones who carry their scars like medals and their silence like shivs. He speaks with a vulgar use of em dashes and ellipses… fuck your style guide, Betty!

This is his first poetry book. It won't be his last (unless he gets black bagged to Pakistan).

The Town That Raised Me Was on Fire Before I Was Born

I was born between a closed church and a Klan sign
neither took me in, but both gave me my name.

Our mayor ran unopposed for twenty years,
said he didn't need votes when fear worked better.

We all learned to whisper in school hallways,
not because of God, but because of coaches
with belt-buckle theology.

The sun never set here
it just got tired of watching the same people get cuffed.
Even the cornfields looked away when it happened.
I once saw a boy's braces catch laces in the gym
he smiled while they kicked him.

They said I was too sensitive.
But I kept the matchbook they used to light him up.
Someday I'll burn this town down
and no one will smell the difference.

WHAT DAD DIDN'T SAY AT THE DINNER TABLE

He never told me he loved me
but he passed the salt like it was holy.
Every night, a silent sermon:
eyes on your plate, hands in your lap,
anger folded into a napkin like bones.

He didn't have to yell
his silence hit like a switch.
Disappointment, his native tongue.
I learned early that fear
doesn't always come with noise.

Once, he nodded when I said I wanted to leave.
That was his blessing.
Or maybe his threat.

Now I trace the shape of that nod
like a scar carved from stillness.

I'm the Question Mark at the End of Every Prayer

I wasn't baptized,
just dunked in expectation and pulled up choking.
The preacher said I'd burn for loving wrong
he didn't ask who I loved, just assumed.

They called it saving my soul.
Felt more like sentencing it.

I asked too many questions in Sunday school.
Why would God flood the earth
but forget to drown the abuser?
Why would Jesus love the sinner
and still sit courtside while I broke?

Every pew knew my name.
They wrote it in the margins of their Bibles
next to the words they used to curse me.

Now I light candles out of spite,
just to watch the wax bleed better than I did.

SMALL ENOUGH TO FIT IN A LOCKER

They shoved me into steel with yesterday's gum,
slurs scribbled in dry erase across my ribs.
The bell rang but no one opened me
just walked past like I was another broken hinge.

I learned to count seconds by holding my breath.
Silence was safer than crying.
Crying got you kicked twice as hard
and quoted Bible verses after.

They said I was a faggot,
but only whispered it when teachers walked by.
Those same teachers called me "distracted,"
as if bruises made good excuses for bad grades.

Sometimes, I still flinch
when I see fluorescent lights and linoleum.
Sometimes, I still shrink
like there's a lock clicking shut behind my name.

They Called It Discipline / I Called It Tuesday

The belt was older than me
cracked leather, holes stretched by fury.
Hung like a crucifix on the closet door.
Stepfather said it was love
but only kissed me through his teeth.

They taught us that pain made men
and that flinching was feminine.
So I learned how to take it
like communion
kneeling, silent, broken-open.

The next morning, mother packed lunch
with the same hands that soaked
my blood soaked shorts.
She didn't look me in the eye.
Didn't need to.

I still smell the leather
when someone says they're doing it for my own good.

When You Finally Learn to Speak, They Call It Yelling

The first time I raised my voice
they said I was angry.
As if quiet had ever protected me.

I tried whispering truth
but they only heard threat.
Tried writing it down
but they burned the page
and said I was lucky they read it at all.

So I sharpened my sentences,
taught my mouth how to bleed.
When I spoke again, it came out
like broken glass in a baptism bowl.

Now they say I'm hostile.
Too loud. Too radical. Too much.
But I've tasted silence
I'd rather die shouting than rot polite.

WE MARCHED UNTIL THE SIDEWALK CRACKED

We made signs from pizza boxes
and broke our voices into chants.
The cops were already sweating
before the sun showed up.

They told us to keep it peaceful
while they loaded rubber bullets.
Said we were disturbing the peace
as if peace wasn't already dead in the streets.

I held hands with a stranger
until the flashbang took our shadows.
Watched him run and drop his inhaler.
I picked it up and ran like it was sacred.

We didn't win that night.
But the sidewalk cracked
where we stood our ground.
Some fractures don't need fixing.

Justice Is Not Blind——It Just Looks Away When It's Paid Enough

I watched a Black boy with a dime bag get sentenced
to more years than he's been alive
while a banker walked free
wallet fat of looted pensions.

A badge testifies better than a mother.
A uniform presses its truth into paper
like God left instructions on the back of a subpoena.

When I yelled in court, they called me contempt.
They cuffed me for tone, not action.
The judge wouldn't look me in the eye
like justice could catch my disease.

They dressed her in marble,
said she was impartial,
but I've seen her blink
for the man who owns the gavel.

She walks in with scales and leaves with stock options.
Lady Justice has a Venmo now.

LIBERTY ENGINE STALLS AT DAWN

I once believed in small government
until I watched it grow teeth
and chew through the lives
of the people I loved.

They called it freedom
but licensed every breath.
Taxed the rain, the steps,
the silence between gunshots.

My neighbor was fined for planting food.
A kid was expelled for the shape of his protest.
They branded rebellion as disorder
and hung our principles on red tape.

Now the engine wheezes,
red, white, and rust.
I tried to fix it once
but every bolt was rigged with a lobbyist.

So I walk now.
Barefoot. Smiling.
At least the ground's still free—
for now.

A Flag Soaking in a Puddle Like Roadkill

I saw it in the gutter
stars wrinkled, stripes dragging like entrails.
Someone had dropped their patriotism
on the way to brunch.

A cop stepped over it.
Didn't flinch.
Didn't salute.

I stood there, watching it soak.
Wondered how many wars it had waved for
and how many names it forgot.

They teach you to fold it
like it's sacred geometry.
To cry when it's burned,
not when it burns people.

But I've buried friends in this country
without a single trumpet.
If that flag is a body,
it died choking on its own pledge.

GOD WEARS A BADGE WHERE I'M FROM

He drives an unmarked SUV
and speaks in citations.
I met Him the night they raided my neighbor's house
for a smell.

He didn't need a warrant
just belief.
And in my town, faith was
whatever let them break your door.

They baptized us with batons.
Said it was for our own good.
Said heaven has a curfew
and only the guilty walk after midnight.

My prayers turned into records.
My records turned into warnings.
The preacher stopped calling my name.
Said I made things political.

But when the gun's pointed at your back,
faith feels like a setup.

I KNOW THE CONSTITUTION BY ITS BRUISES

It was taught like gospel
Bill of Rights in laminated sheets,
recited like scripture
with hands on hearts
and eyes on the principal.

But no one read me Miranda
when I was sixteen and mouthy.
No one protected my papers
when they opened my locker
and found shame scrawled on lined paper.

They said freedom wasn't free
I didn't know the cost was my silence,
my sweat,
my body flattened against a cruiser
while my ID shook in my hand
like it was already guilty.

You learn fast that "liberty"
is mostly paperwork and loopholes.
And bruises don't vote.

DEAD FLAGS DON'T BURN

I tried once.
Lit the corner with a cigarette lighter
I'd stolen from a cop's pregnant teen princess.
But it fizzled like all things sacred.

The fabric was treated.
Fireproof, just like the lie.
Red doesn't bleed when it's printed in bulk.
White doesn't stain.
Blue only bruises others.

It just stared at me,
soaking in heat,
refusing to disappear.

That's the thing about dead symbols,
they don't scream.
They don't decay.
They just hang
like reminders of what we were supposed to become.

And when they finally fall,
it's not justice.
It's gravity.

THE REVOLUTION WAS UNFRIENDED BY ALGORITHM

We organized in comment threads
until the bots outnumbered us.
Planned a march in DMs
that vanished with the sunrise.

They said shadow
bans weren't real—
but I haven't been seen in months.
My posts turn to ash mid-scroll.
My grief gets flagged for review.

There's a folder somewhere,
where my face is stored next to "radical."
Where my IP bleeds across
ten thousand red-flagged keywords.

I wanted to change the world.
But all I changed
was my password.

And even that
felt like surrender.

Everyone I Loved Died Screaming or Voting

We lost Tyler to tear gas.
Not from the blast,
but the breath he didn't take fast enough.
Ash in his lungs like a final ballot.

And Maria—
she voted like it was magic,
like she believed the booth was a confessional.
They gerrymandered her into silence.
Said she didn't count,
but still sent ads to her grave.

We light candles for the ones
who bled for a system
that drinks them dry,
then mails condolences
postage due.

Democracy is a tomb
with velvet curtains.
We scream into it,
praying the echo sounds like empathy.

No One Here Gets Out Divine

I used to think survival was sacred.
Now I just think it's luck.

They told me I was made in God's image
but I've seen His mugshot.
He looks like a landlord
and smells like rubber gloves.

I lost my faith in a voting booth
with broken glass for curtains.
It cut my hand when I touched the screen,
and I bled liberal and still lost.

These days, I pray only in code.
Just in case someone's listening
who knows what mercy feels like.

But even the angels are freelancers now.
And heaven's paywall
just went up again.

Protestor Danced While the Gas Hit Her Skin

She didn't flinch
when the canister rolled at her feet.
Just spun—barefoot, bleeding—like the gas was perfume
and the cops were stagehands.

I watched from behind a barricade
of cardboard and cowardice.
She locked eyes with a riot shield
and laughed.

Not manic.
Not brave.
Just done.

We all knew what it meant—
that moment where resistance
stops asking for results
and becomes the ritual.

They arrested her
for disturbing the peace.
But she danced like the war was over
and she'd already won.

Silence Tastes Like Choice

I lied about the pills—
just wanted silence to taste like choice.
They found me curled next to a copy
of the Constitution with all the rights ripped out.

I stopped praying when I realized
He only listened to people who look like cops.
Stopped speaking when I realized
words are admissible in court but not in love.

There's a kind of silence
that smells like bleach and gunmetal.
A kind that lets you sleep through gunshots
but wake up screaming at sunlight.

People say I should talk more.
But what's a voice if it doesn't indict?
What's healing if it makes you soft?
I'd rather stay broken than forgive my captors.

I Wrote My Name on the Police Report

They asked for my statement
while my hands still shook
from the grip of steel and doubt.

Said I could press charges,
but only if I had the right kind of bruises.
The kind that photograph well.
The kind that match their forms.

So I lit a cigarette
with the intake sheet
and wrote my name in the haze.

Said I was present. Said I existed.

They filed the report
under "uncooperative."
Said the story didn't add up.
That's the thing about trauma—
it's never arithmetic.

And some names were only ever meant
to be written in smoke.

EVERYTHING I CARRIED WAS A WARNING

A lighter.
A folded flyer from a march no one showed up for.
A copy of the Bill of Rights, redacted in highlighter.
My father's silence, still ringing.
My mother's fists, packed small.

I carried pepper spray
and a picture of myself smiling—
just in case they needed something
for the evening news.

Every scar in my backpack.
Every exit strategy etched into the sole of my boots.
A knife hidden in a library card.
A manifesto I never finished.

They say I should let it go.
But I've never dropped anything
without bleeding for it.

And some of us were born
with warning labels instead of birthmarks.

SOME PRAYERS ONLY WORK IF YOU BLEED FIRST

Knees on tile,
hands cracked open like old books.
I mouthed the words they taught me
in Sunday school
but changed the names.

They said ask and you shall receive—
so I asked for peace
and got tased.
Asked for mercy
and got the boot pressed on me.

Turns out, salvation is means-tested.
You need the right ZIP code
and a clean record
and the decency not to die on camera.

The only prayers that reached heaven
came soaked in pain.
And even then,
God sent an automatic reply.

How Quiet Became a Weapon

I stopped speaking the year
they started quoting me in reports.
Stopped testifying the moment
my words were filtered through fear.

Now my silence is strategic.
It has edges.
It waits.

I enter rooms like smoke.
Not unseen—
but ungraspable.

When they ask where I stand,
I stare.
When they ask what I think,
I blink.

This is not surrender.
This is siege.

I've seen what noise gets you.
Now I watch them unravel
under the weight
of everything I do not say.

Anatomy of a Riot

First, a breath held too long—
lungs swollen with names no one read.

Then a knee.
A slur.
A cracked tooth mistaken for progress.

Next, the march.
The cardboard sign soaked in spit.
The chant that starts soft
ends in sirens.

Followed by fire.
Not literal
just the kind that burns from the inside
and knows how to wait.

Then the stillness.
The coverage.
The spin.
The justifications pinned to memory
like a participation ribbon for grief.

Last comes the forgetting.
But not for us.
We become the match.

The crowd.
The cost.

This is how a riot lives—
not in broken windows,
but in the people who never
walked away...

Afterword

If you made it this far, I hope your hands are shaking.

Not from fear, but from the weight of recognition—of rage reflected, of memories you weren't sure had names until now. This book isn't just a collection of poems. It's a manual. A mirror. A Molotov. And now it's yours.

Don't let anyone shame you for how you feel. Don't let the world convince you that your grief is too loud or your anger too inconvenient. **You're not broken**—you're alive in a system that profits from pretending you aren't.

So get loud. Organize. March. Build coalitions. Tear down bad laws. Run for office. Paint the signs. Start the zine. Be the whistleblower. Slam your name into the ballot box like a fist through glass.

Whatever you do, don't be silent.

And don't stand still.

The riot doesn't end on the page.

You are the next verse.

— *Evan McMahon*

Also by Evan McMahon

POETRY

Anatomy of a Riot *(the book in your hand)*

Cookies & Collaborators *(August 2025)*

Muzzle Velocity *(October 2025)*

The fyp Revolutionary *(December 2025)*